D1548641

DAVID C. DRISKELL

Artist, Educator, Author

*Maine Art Series for Young Readers
and for Art Students of All Ages*

PAT DAVIDSON REEF

DAVID C. DRISKELL: ARTIST, EDUCATOR, AUTHOR
BY PAT DAVIDSON REEF
Maine Art Series for Young Readers

Copyright © 2020 Pat Davidson Reef

ISBN: 978-1-63381-212-3

All rights reserved. With the exception of short excerpts for critical reviews, no part of this work may be reproduced or transmitted in any form or by any means whatsoever without permission in writing from the publisher.

On the cover:
Festival Thelma by David C. Driskell, woodcut, black & white, 1966, photo courtesy Driskell Center

Opposite title page:
David C. Driskell in his Maine studio, photo courtesy Rodney Moore

Designed and produced by:
Maine Authors Publishing
Thomaston, Maine 04861
www.maineauthorspublishing.com

Printed in the United States of America

DEDICATIONS

*For my parents, Sally and David D. Davidson, who were
wonderful role models in my life, and for my two daughters, Grace and Heidi;
my five grandchildren, Courtney, Toby, Megan, Jamie, and Ryan;
and my two great-grandchildren, Juliette and baby Adam.*

A special dedication to my grandson, Adam Berkowitz, whom I will always carry in my heart.

WITH LOVE

ACKNOWLEDGMENTS

*A special thank-you to David Driskell, who generously allowed me to interview him and gave
me permission to use photos of specific works and personal photos of family. He passed away as we
went to press, a sorrowful loss that has made this book a tribute as much as a celebration of his life.*

*Also a special thanks to Rodney Moore, who provided many photos of works for this book, and
the Driskell Center, who generously sent immediate photos.*

*In addition, a special thank-you to Connie Reagan, who converted my Pages document into
Microsoft Word so it would be compatible with Adobe InDesign. Another thank-you to Tom
Berman, who helped create a folder for all Driskell research to be kept in. And a very special
thank-you to Avis Smith, who helped edit this book.*

*Last but not least is a special thank-you to Gael McKibben and Nancy Payson, who encouraged
me to follow a dream and make it a reality—this book.*

Maine studio

"When I come to Maine, time stops," said David Driskell in a lecture at the Portland Museum of Art. "Maine has that way of captivating you."

David Driskell is a nationally known artist, author, and educator. He has lived in Maine for over 57 years in the summertime and has another home in Maryland, where he taught art at the University of Maryland, College Park, for 22 years.

David was born in 1931 in Eatonton, Georgia. He is the son of a minister and the grandson of a slave. He came to Maine in 1953 as a student/participant in the Skowhegan School of Painting and Sculpture. Over the years, he became a faculty member there and was placed on both the Board of Governors and the Board of Trustees of the Skowhegan School. Falling in love with Maine, he bought a home in 1961 in Falmouth and brought his family. His wife, Thelma, and two daughters, Daviryne and Daphne, love Maine, too. They visit David with their children every summer.

Driskell Family ▶

Although David is known for his abstract work, he has also done representational work. An outstanding realistic work is **Festival Thelma**, a black-and-white woodcut of his wife that was created in 1966 and can be seen on the cover of this book.

Another representational work is titled **Green Chair**, an acrylic on canvas. This work is realistic, but David begins to explore different ways of seeing. He draws from real objects, but his arrangement of space begins to be abstract.

Representational art shows realistic images as we see them in real life.

Abstract art does not attempt to record reality. This style uses shapes, forms, colors, and textures for their own beauty.

Green Chair ➤

Vines and Trees

The Driskell family home in Maine is located under cathedral pine trees. David created a studio nearby, where he works every morning. Outside the studio he created a beautiful flower and vegetable garden. When he is in Maine he likes to work in it.

As a child David loved to draw. He often sketched in a sketchbook. In fact, as an adult, he carries a sketchbook with him so that he can capture any sight that moves him.

Here is a sketch from his sketchbook that is semi-abstract, depicting tall trees with vines created with a black Conté crayon, an especially hard pencil used for drawing.

The artist has focused on forms in nature in intricate patterns. It is a fascinating work.

◀ *Vines and Trees*

David loves nature, and it is very important in his life. When he moved to Maine, he loved the smell of pine trees and the Maine earth in his garden. Pine trees became a subject in many of his paintings.

Important themes in David's work are flowers and nature. Flowers in pots and hanging green plants can be seen all over his home.

"Flowers bring us joy, and they connect us to the beauty of nature in a special way. Our love for flowers expresses our love for the joy of creation," David said.

Walking down the driveway of David's home in Maine, one can see his garden with orange daylilies and black-eyed Susans on one side and pine trees on the other side. Through the pine trees you can see a small brook. The natural beauty of Maine surrounds his home and studio.

Family is very important to David. On the next page is an image of his ten-year-old grandson, Darius, created in a woodcut in 1989.

◀ *Still Life on Table*

Darius

Darius   Ab   Arisksll 82

*A*familiar theme that David likes to paint is the Maine pine tree. Notice that he is beginning to leave representational art.

Driskell said, "Maine has influenced my work in many ways. I love the pine trees here and the state's natural beauty. I love gardening around my home and studio in Falmouth, where I live in the summer. When I come to Maine, I can relax and have privacy. Maine's natural environment gives me new energy."

"When I come to Maine, things change. I bring to Maine my experiences in life, masks, and African-American culture, as well as my love of nature in Maine, which has a strong impact on me and can be seen in my work."

◀ *Pine and Moon*

Bakota Girl I

Another important theme that David explores is African culture. You can see his style is changing to exciting abstract forms with geometric and overlapping shapes in this wonderful woodcut titled **Bakota Girl I**.

Woodcuts are carved on a block of prepared wood. Ink or paint is rolled over the wood, and paper is pressed down on the carved ink or painted image. The work of art is created on paper from this process. The wood block itself is crossed out or destroyed. The art is what remains on the paper.

In a woodcut, each color has to be applied separately. **Bakota Girl I** has many colors, so it took many printings to make this one image.

African images can be seen in many of David's works. In fact, David Driskell is a leading international authority on African-American culture. After retiring in 1998 from teaching art at the University of Maryland, the school created in his honor the David C. Driskell Center for the Study of the Visual Arts and Culture of African Americans and African Diaspora in 2001.

Driskell has been one of the primary people responsible for bringing African-American art into the mainstream of American society through his own artwork, writing, and teaching, and by curating exhibits by artists of color.

A wonderful aspect of David's own paintings and graphic arts is that his work includes so many symbols and intricate patterns. Familiar symbols include plants, fish, biblical themes, pine trees, sun, flowers, and masked spiritual images overlapping each other in space, like the work **Spirits Watching**, a hand-colored offset lithograph.

Driskell said, "Masks are a universal creative representation of people expressing their joys and fears about life."

"In African masks, the image is centered on the face or the head. It is felt that the head reveals the seat of wisdom in African thought. African-American artists often use masks in their art to represent a connection to Africa, their ancestral home. Some masks are symbols of joy, sorrow, and spiritual connection to past generations. Masks convey another dimension of life."

◀ *Spirits Watching*

riskell's work reflects spirituality. He has said, "Religion and ritual and the mythic are concerns I have always nurtured."

A beautiful spiritual work can be seen in the round stained glass window reproduced on this page. In 1991, he was asked to create stained glass window designs for the Peoples Congregational United Church of Christ in Washington, DC. Two designs were created, one for the east window and one for the west window. At right is the design for the east window.

Inside the round window is the image of a slave running back to Africa, a wishful desire of many slaves first brought to America. The figure has a halo because he has accepted Christianity.

Stained glass windows are a unique art form. They were originally designed for churches in the Renaissance to teach stories of the Bible.

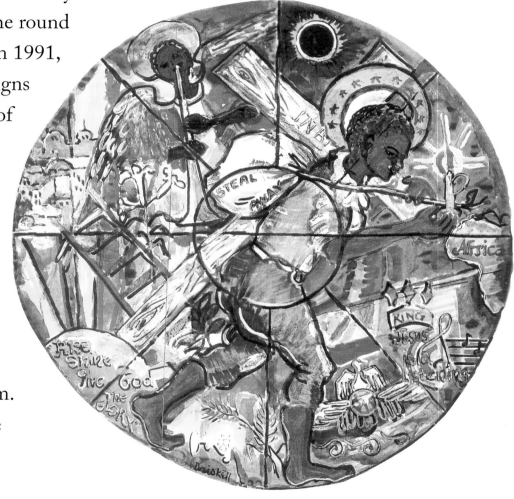

Study for the east window, Peoples Congregational United Church of Christ, Washington, DC

David learned to do stained glass window designs at Howard University under James Porter, an important mentor. Porter had introduced stained glass window design in his mural classes. He made students experiment with wax paper and crayons.

Years later, in 1996, David was asked to design 65 stained glass windows for the DeForest Chapel, located on the grounds of Talladega College in Alabama. The stained glass windows, which he designed at Talladega, represented disciplines of study and African-American history offered at the college.

Musical symbols, masks, and flowers were some of the designs created for the windows which allowed light to come into the building.

Photo of installation of east window, Peoples Congregational United Church of Christ, Washington, DC

Bible stories read in David's home when he was a child inspired him to love the stories in the Bible. Spiritual themes can be seen in many of his works. Here is a work depicting Jonah in the whale, a subject from the Old Testament.

◀ *Jonah in the Whale*

When David was a child, television, computers, and cell phones did not exist. He read books and shared them with his family. Storytelling in the family took the place of television. He grew up hearing stories from the Bible and sketched in his spare time. Going to school was important. David got a scholarship to Howard University, graduating in 1955, and a scholarship to Catholic University, where he received a Master of Fine Arts degree in 1962. David met his wife, Thelma, when he was at Howard University in 1951. They were married in 1952. **School Life, David and Thelma** was the first portrait David created of Thelma and himself.

School Life, David and Thelma

Music is an inspiration for David as he paints. He has a radio in his studio and likes to hear music while creating. A favorite musician is Wynton Marsalis.

Jazz Singer (Lady of Leisure, Fox) is a beautiful oil painting and collage done in 1974. It is an image of a woman singing in many ranges as the semi-abstract painting captures the sounds of the unwritten notes that are found in impromptu interludes of jazz.

◀ *Jazz Singer (Lady of Leisure, Fox)*

*D*riskell is not only an artist; he is also an author. He has written over 40 monographs on African-American artists and is the author of such major works as *Two Centuries of Black American Art 1750–1950*, published by Knopf (1976); *Hidden Heritage: African American Art 1800–1950*, published by the Art Association of America (1986); *African American Aesthetics: A Post Modernist View*, edited by Driskell and published by the Smithsonian Institution Press (1995); and *Evolution: Five Decades of Printmaking by David C. Driskell*, published by Pomegranate

Communications (2007), in which Driskell explains the printing process.

Below is an example of an offset lithograph print, **Ancestral Images, The Forest**. It is characteristic of David's style. On the following pages are other examples of his work to explore.

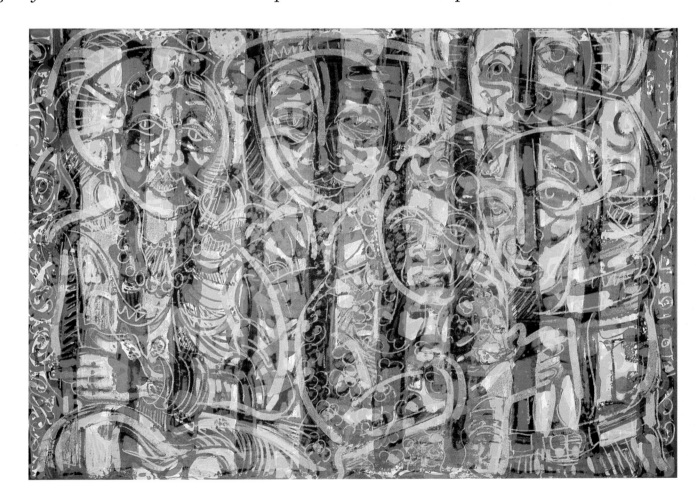

Ancestral Images, The Forest ▶

"Pure art always comes from a voice within and is a surging element of our common humanity."
—David Driskell

"Creativity connects us from one generation to another."

—DAVID DRISKELL

Bakota Girl II ▶

◀ Banners Condomble

"Through a realization of creativity we can see the past and the future."

—David Driskell

This work was influenced by David's mother's strip quilt style, which he saw as a child and re-created in an abstract work of art.

Bahain Lace ▶

"Art transcends time. It allows us to have a common connection."

—David Driskell

"In **Ghetto Wall #2**, I have attempted to show aspects of history as revealed in the Civil Rights Movement as they apply to the whole of American society. African-American history is an important part of our national voice, and the symbols of the star, the flag, and the wall below all help to tell our American story."

◀ *Ghetto Wall #2*

David Driskell has won so many awards that it is impossible to list them all in this book. However, three significant awards are The National Humanities Medal given by President Bill Clinton in 2000, The Skowhegan School of Painting and Sculpture Lifetime Legacy Award given in 2016 at the Plaza Hotel in New York, and the prestigious Cummings Award for Artistic Excellence at the Colby College Museum of Art, July 8, 2017.

In addition, the University of Maryland honored David by naming a building and an educational institute after him, the David C. Driskell Center for the Study of Visual Arts and Culture of African Americans and African Diaspora. In 2018, David was elected as a Fellow to the American Academy of Arts and Letters.

We in Maine are lucky to have such an important artist, scholar, writer, and educator living among us and sharing his views.

"Art allows us to have a creative voice."
—DAVID DRISKELL

David painting in studio ▶

The Voice of the Artist

AN INTERVIEW WITH DAVID DRISKELL
by Pat Davidson Reef

If you could give advice to a young art student today, what would you say?

Read about artists and their lives and go to museums and artists' exhibitions as often as you can. Study your chosen craft and work hard to perfect it.

At what age did you start to draw? What materials did you use?

I began drawing and using crayons when I was six years old, but my family could not afford to buy art supplies for me. So I improvised and used brown paper bags and discarded magazine pages to draw upon.

Who were your mentors?

My father was—in addition to being a minister, a carpenter, and a stonemason. He built our little house of stones in Appalachia in western North Carolina in the woods near a creek. I watched him make furniture, and I saw my mother make strip quilts and straw bulrush baskets. They became my first teachers. Upon entering college, I had a number of mentors: James A. Porter, Lois M. Jones, and James L. Wells, among others. Later, I made the acquaintance of Romare Bearden, Charles White, Jacob Lawrence, Elizabeth Catlett, and Willard W. Cummings (Bill). They became my mentors, and I collected their art.

You work in many forms of media. What media do you prefer?

I prefer to work in gouache (an opaque watercolor medium), collage, and encaustic (a wax-base paint) and oils.

What place does the environment have in your work?

I am always moved by the beauty of nature wherever I travel or live. I am always trying to help preserve nature in its natural state, and I prefer helping native plants thrive naturally. I like gardening in Maine because I am able to use many native plants in a garden setting.

What do you think is the responsibility of the artist?
To make the public aware of beauty or aware of social justice, or both?

The artist has the dual responsibility of creating a new vision of the world by inventing and expanding upon what we see and by creating beauty as a desirable quality of life. The artist should be able to make us aware of the good life by asking for social justice for all.

Do children need an art teacher or an art school? Can young people learn on their own?
Do artists need each other to share ideas?

All artists learn from past artists. Not everyone would like to be an artist. But art schools and art teachers are a must for those who wish to become professional artists. Some artists are self-taught, but they always learn from interacting with each other.

Who are your favorite artists?

I have too many favorite artists to list them here. But I love ancient art, Renaissance and modern art, as well as contemporary art being created today.

Are sketchbooks important to all artists? Why do you like to work in sketchbooks?

I have used sketchbooks over the years to keep an account of my travels and make sketches of scenes I may wish to re-create later. The sketchbook for me is the bread and butter of a planned meal in art.

What is more important to an artist: a museum exhibit, a gallery show, encouragement from home, or communication with other artists?

All artists should study all forms of art available to them in order to be made aware of art history and the role art has played in civilization. Museum exhibits help an artist establish one's standing as a professional. Gallery shows inform museums [about] what is available. Encouragement from all sources gives the artist self-confidence.

APPENDIX A: GLOSSARY

Abstract art: works that do not attempt to record reality. This style uses shapes, forms, colors, and textures for their own beauty

Acrylic: a form of paint with synthetic resins that dries quickly

Bulrush basket: handwoven basket from a flat surface water plant, a grass used in weaving

Continent: a continuous tract of land. Africa is a continent with 53 countries in it. Asia is a continent. North America is a continent with the United States in it

Collage: a work of art made by gluing different materials onto its surface, like pieces of paper or fabric or photographs

Collagraph: a print made by building up a surface creating recessed areas

Diaspora: spread of any people from their original homeland

Encaustic: a process of painting using pigments mixed with hot wax and dry pigment

Gouache: method of painting using opaque pigments ground in water and thickened with a glue-like substance

Linocut: a design or form carved in relief on a block of linoleum

Lithography: a process of printing from a flat surface treated to repel the ink except where it is required for printing

Monograph: a detailed study of a specific subject often published in a book similar to a catalogue or a journal

Oil paints: a form of paint with an oil base; has thick texture but dries slowly. It is easier to use than watercolors because images stay as painted

Offset lithograph: a print that is not made from original plates; it is transferred to another surface and then printed

Stained glass window: colored glass used to form decorative designs that are connected with a lead framework similar to a mosaic; often used in churches

Watercolor: a form of paint with a water base. Paler colors can be created by adding water, not white. Control of water on the paintbrush determines the quality of work

Woodcut: a print that is made from a design cut into a block of wood. Ink is rolled over it, and the image pressed onto the paper is the work of art in reverse when printed

APPENDIX B:
BIOGRAPHICAL INFORMATION

Born: Eatonton, Georgia, June 7, 1931

Died: Washington, DC, April 1, 2020

Parents: Reverend G.W. Driskell and Mary Lou Cloud Driskell

Wife: Thelma

Children: Daphne and Daviryne

Education: Howard University, 1955; Catholic University, Master of Fine Art, 1962

ACADEMIC POSITIONS

1955–1962: Assistant Professor of Art, Talladega College, Talladega, Alabama

1962–1966: Associate Professor of Art, Howard University, Washington, DC

1966–1976: Professor of Art, Fisk University, Nashville, Tennessee

1973: Spring term Visiting Professor, Bowdoin College, Brunswick, Maine

1973: Visiting Professor, Bates College, Lewiston, Maine

1975 and 1992: Printmaking Instructor, Haystack Mountain School of Crafts, Deer Isle, Maine

1977–1998: Professor of Art, University of Maryland, College Park, Maryland

1978: Resident Faculty member, Skowhegan School of Painting and Sculpture, Skowhegan, Maine.

1989: Distinguished Visiting Scholar, Queens College, City University of New York, Flushing, New York

2004: Faculty, Maine Art Education Workshops, Haystack Mountain School of Crafts, Deer Isle, Maine

◀ Driskell Family

"What we leave as proof of our being here will not necessarily be in the sciences, in politics, in economics, but will manifest itself through the arts."

—David Driskell

◀ *The Young Herbalist*

APPENDIX C: BIBLIOGRAPHY

Childs, Adrienne. *Evolution: Five Decades of Printmaking by David C. Driskell*. Pomegranate Communications, 2008.

Creative Spirit: The Art of David C. Driskell. Text contributions by David C. Driskell, Robert Steele, Floyd Coleman, Adrienne Childs, and Julie McGee. Maryland State Arts Council and David C. Driskell Center for the Study of Visual Arts and Culture of African Americans and the African Diaspora, 2011.

Driskell, David C. *In Search of Creative Truth* (DVD), produced and directed by Richard Kane, co-produced by Bruce Brown; part of the Maine Masters Project sponsored by the Union of Maine Visual Artists; © 2012 Kane-Lewis productions, www.kanelewis.com.

———, editor. *African American Visual Aesthetics: A Post Modern View*. Smithsonian Institution, 1995.

———. *Contemporary Visual Expressions*. Anacostia Neighborhood Museum of the Smithsonian Institution, 1987.

———. *Hidden Heritage: African American Art 1850–1950*. Bellevue Museum of Art, 1985.

———. *Paintings Across the Decade 1996–2006*. Introduction by Lowry Stokes Sims; interview by Bruce Brown: D.C. Moore Gallery, New York, 1996.

———. Driskell quotes used on pages 18–22, from lecture at the University of Southern Maine sponsored by the Portland Museum of Art, August 22, 2019.

———. *Two Centuries of Black American Art*. Los Angeles Museum and Knopf, 1976.

Keyes, Bob. "New Community Space in Portland Will Create Support for Artists of Color." *Portland Press Herald*, Portland, Maine, January 2, 2019.

McGee, Julie. *David C. Driskell, Artist and Scholar*. Pomegranate Communications, 2006.

Reef, Patricia Davidson. "Artist David C. Driskell Creates His Own Vision of What He Sees." *Sun Journal*, Lewiston, Maine, December 1, 2009.

———. "Biennial Exhibit, Portland Museum of Art: David C. Driskell." *Sun Journal*, February 6, 2018.

———. Book review of *Evolution: Five Decades of Printmaking by David Driskell* by Adrienne Childs, editor. *Journal Tribune*, Biddeford, Maine, September 14, 2019.

APPENDIX D: PHOTO AND ART CREDITS

Cover: David C. Driskell

Festival Thelma

Woodcut, black & white, 1966

13.5 inches diameter

Photo courtesy Driskell Center

P. ii: Photo of David seated inside Maine studio

with art supplies in background

Photo courtesy Rodney Moore

P. vi: Photo of Maine studio, outside

Photo courtesy Rodney Moore

P. 1: Photo of David seated inside studio

with art work on canvas behind him

Photo courtesy Rodney Moore

P. 2: Photo of Driskell Family

Daviryne (daughter), David, Thelma (wife),

Daphne (daughter)

Photo courtesy Rodney Moore

P. 3: David C. Driskell

Green Chair

Acrylic on canvas, 1978

40 x 24 inches

Photo courtesy Rodney Moore

P. 4: David C. Driskell

Vines and Trees

Conté crayon, 2017

14 x 11 inches

Photo courtesy Rodney Moore

P. 5:   David C. Driskell

Maine Landscape with Pines

Woodcut/linocut, 1971

10.5 inches diameter

Photo courtesy Rodney Moore

P. 6:   David C. Driskell

Still Life on Table

Hand-colored woodcut, 2000

11 x 8.75 inches

Photo courtesy Driskell Center

P. 7:   David C. Driskell

Darius

Woodcut, 1982

10.75 x 8.95 inches

Photo courtesy Driskell Center

P. 8:   David C. Driskell

Pine and Moon

Oil on masonite, 1971

47.375 x 35.125 inches

Portland Museum of Art

Museum purchase with support from

    the Friends of the Collection, 2011.4

Image courtesy Pillar Digital Imaging

Copyright David C. Driskell

P. 9:   David C. Driskell

Bakota Girl I

Woodcut, color, 1974

18.75 x 12.5 inches

Photo courtesy Driskell Center

P. 10:   Photo of David in Studio

Photo courtesy Rodney Moore

P. 11:   David C. Driskell

Spirits Watching

Hand-colored lithograph, 1986

21.5 x 30 inches

Photo courtesy Driskell Center

18.5 x 12.5 inches

Photo courtesy Driskell Center

P. 20:   David C. Driskell

Bahain Lace

Oil and collage on canvas, 1988

43 x 38 inches

Photo courtesy Driskell Center

P. 21:   David C. Driskell

Ghetto Wall #2

Oil, acrylic, and collage on linen, 1970

60 x 50 inches

Portland Museum of Art

Museum purchase with support from the Emily
     Eaton Moore and Family Fund for the
     Collection, The Homburger Endowment
     for Acquisitions, and the Friends of the Art
     Collection, 2019/16

Image courtesy the artist and the
     D.C. Moore Gallery

Copyright David C. Driskell

P. 22:   Photo of David painting in studio

Photo courtesy Rodney Moore

P. 28:   Photo of Driskell family

David, Rodney Moore (nephew), Daviryne
(daughter), Thelma (wife), Daphne (daughter)

Photo courtesy Julie McGee

P. 29:   David C. Driskell

The Young Herbalist, self-portrait of the artist

Color lithograph, 2000

24 x 18.25 inches

Photo courtesy Rodney Moore

P. 36:   David C. Driskell

General Store at Cundy's Harbor, Maine

Pen and ink, 2009

7 x 10 inches

Photo courtesy Rodney Moore

APPENDIX F: DRISKELL WORKS IN PROFESSIONAL COLLECTIONS

National

Baltimore Museum of Art, Baltimore, Maryland

Birmingham Museum of Art, Birmingham, Alabama

Greenville County Museum of Art, Greenville, South Carolina

National Gallery of Art, Washington, DC

National Museum of African American History and Culture, Smithsonian Institution, Washington, DC

Smithsonian Museum of American Art, Washington DC

Maine

Bates College Museum of Art, Lewiston, Maine

Bowdoin College Museum of Art, Brunswick, Maine

Colby College Museum of Art, Waterville, Maine

Farnsworth Museum, Rockland, Maine

Portland Museum of Art, Portland, Maine

General Store at Cundy's Harbor, Maine

APPENDIX E: AWARDS AND HONORS

1964: Museum Donor Award, American Federation of Arts

1981: Distinguished Alumni Award for Academic Achievement in Art and Education, Howard University, Washington, DC

1986: Governor's Award, Skowhegan School of Painting and Sculpture in honor of scholarship and curatorial practices

2000: National Humanities Award presented by President Bill Clinton, Washington, DC

2001: University of Maryland honors David by naming a building and an educational institute after him: the David C. Driskell Center for the Study of Visual Arts and Culture of African Americans and African Diaspora

2002: Frederick Douglas Award, University of Maryland, College Park, Maryland

2002: MECA Award for National Leadership, Maine College of Art, Portland, Maine

2004: High Museum of Art, Atlanta, Georgia, establishes annual David C. Driskell Prize

2006: Brandywine Achievement Award, Brandywine Workshop, Philadelphia, Pennsylvania

2016: National Art Education Association Annual Award, New York

2016: Skowhegan School of Painting and Sculpture Lifetime Legacy Award, Plaza Hotel, New York

2017: Cummings Award for Artistic Excellence, Colby College, Waterville, Maine

2018: Elected to the American Academy of Arts and Letters